Chefs' Special

Low Calorie Desserts

Chefs' Special

Low Calorie Desserts

Mallika Nagarajan

Lustre Press
Roli Books

Low-calorie Treats

Dieting is not a one-time exercise. People with weight problems usually have to be careful about what they eat all their lives, and have to change their habits and lifestyles in order to remain healthy and trim. If controlling one's weight is going to be a lifetime activity, then it should be exciting and fun. Cooking is one of the most creative of artistic activities, where different colours, flavours, textures and ideas intermingle to create a masterpiece! Diet food is no different.

This book is an attempt to create desserts which are low calorie yet luscious enough to satisfy all those sinful cravings. The key to a successful diet is the motivation required to adhere to it. And the best way to remain motivated is to be innovative with the food you eat.

While it is written primarily for those on a diet, people who don't have a weight problem will also love the easy-to-make variety of low-calorie desserts and delicious beverages and shakes given in the book. After all, good health is one's most important asset. These recipes cut down on unhealthy fats and sugars and provide the healthy alternative.

Dedication

To my mother, Dr Shanta Nagarajan

Tips for Easy Weight Loss

- If you are serious about losing weight, invest in a kitchen scale and measuring cups and spoons. Remember to weigh and measure everything you eat.

- Buy a calorie counter and nutritional value book and be aware of what you eat.

- Check with a dietitian about your allotted calorie intake and strictly follow it.

- Incorporate a lot of fibre in your food in the form of wholewheat flour, wheat bran, fresh fruits and vegetables.

- While artificial sweetener is a boon for anyone with a sweet tooth, it is much better to ultimately eat natural, wholesome products. You can substitute half or more of the sweetener in the recipes with sugar – but do it according to your calorie allotment – and remember sugar adds as much as 20 calories per tsp!

- Eat desserts which are less sweet.

- Use fruits or fruit purées to sweeten the food. Jaggery, honey and unrefined sugars are healthier alternatives.

- Reduce the fat content, avoid fried foods. Fat adds 45 calories per tsp. Eat low cholesterol fats like refined oils if possible. Nutritionists, today, do not recommend a completely fat-free diet – this leads to problems including hair loss. Fat contains vitamins A, D and E and is essential for metabolism. A little fat in the form of oil, nuts, etc., is essential. The Indian Council of Medical Research recommends a daily energy intake of around 3-6% of fat as essential.

- Avoid over cooking the food. Eat uncooked fruits and vegetables, or cook them slightly.

- Enhance low-calorie foods with flavourful spices, condiments, essences and creativity.

- Garnish and present the food well – it makes a big difference. Also experiment with different combinations of textures, flavours, and yes, even temperatures.

- Combine exercise with dieting. Walking is one of the best exercises one can do.

How to Use Your Oven

- Learn to recognise the individual personality of your oven!
- Turn the top or bottom burner on or off if the cake cooks too slow or fast.
- Cover the cake with a sheet of foil if it browns too quickly.
- Bake in the middle shelf, unless instructed otherwise, as in meringues to get best results.
- Use evenly greased and floured baking tins.
- Even if the baking time is given, observe and test the cake to see if it is done.
- The cake is done when the top is firm and golden, and a toothpick inserted into the centre of the cake comes out clean.
- To preheat the oven whenever instructed to do so, switch it on and leave the door open for around 5-10 minutes.

Beating Egg Whites – Just Right!

These are some useful tips that one should keep in mind while beating egg whites and meringues:

- Use a copper or metal bowl washed with soap, rubbed with lemon and rinsed with water to remove traces of grease. Dry with a soft, clean cloth.

- Put the egg whites in the prepared bowl making sure that they do not contain any yolk, shell, etc.

- Follow the same procedure with the beater blades; wash, rub with lemon, rinse and dry.

- Beat the egg whites with a pinch of salt and cream of tartar for best results. The egg whites must be at room temperature.

- Use an electric beater to beat the egg whites. Start with a slow speed and beat till the whites turn creamy. Then add 2 tsp of sugar, per egg white. Now beat at high speed till the whites resemble whipped cream and form stiff peaks. Add the rest of the sugar or artificial sweetener and beat further for a minute till the sugar dissolves. To fold the egg whites into a cake mixture, first mix a couple of spoons of the egg white to the heavier mixture to lighten it. Then fold in the rest, a little at a time, with a metal spoon or a rubber spatula.

- For meringues, preheat the oven at around 225°C. Place the meringue mixture on the topmost shelf, and bake for 4-5 minutes or till the meringue is delicately coloured and crisp on top.

Medium Calorie Fruits

Wherever fruits are required use in the following order of preference. If you need to use anything in addition, check out the calories first.

- Melons are available in two colours – white or red. However, the white melon is preferred in cooking.
- Papaya gives a creamy texture whether ground, puréed or cooked.
- Fresh figs, strawberries, oranges, grapefruits, pineapples and loquats.
- Apples.
- Guavas, peaches, apricots, plums, pears and cherries.
- Grapes. The green grapes are a little higher in calorie than the blue ones.
- Pomegranates.
- Bananas.
- Mangoes.

Basic Recipes

■ Sponge Cake

Calories per serving: approx. 130

Take 100 gm refined flour (*maida*), 4½ gm baking powder, 1½ gm soda bicarbonate, 4 large eggs, 50 gm powdered sugar, 3-4 drops vanilla essence and 15 ml vinegar (*sirka*).

Grease a 7″-8″ baking tin and dust lightly with flour. Sift the flour with baking powder and soda bicarbonate. Keep aside. Beat the eggs with powdered sugar over a pan of hot water till thick and creamy. Carefully fold in the flour mixture into the egg mixture a few tbsp at a time, adding 1-3 tbsp of water, if necessary, to obtain a dropping consistency. Stir in the vanilla essence and vinegar. Bake at 150°C for 30-35 minutes or until the cake is well risen and golden and a toothpick inserted in the centre comes out clean.

VARIATIONS

Strawberry Sponge Cake: Add 3-4 drops strawberry (*istabari*) essence to the sponge cake.

Orange Sponge Cake: Add 2-3 drops orange (*santra*) essence, 1 tsp grated orange peel and 2-3 tbsp fresh orange juice instead of water to the sponge cake.

Chocolate Sponge Cake: Remove 1 tbsp refined flour (*maida*) and add 1 tbsp cocoa powder instead to the sponge cake.

■ Whipped Cream
Calories per serving: approx. 210

Take 10 gm cornflour, 100 ml skimmed milk, 100 gm cottage cheese (*paneer*) made from skimmed milk, 2-3 drops vanilla essence, 20 gm artificial sweetener or to taste and water to blend.

Dissolve the cornflour in skimmed milk; cook till it thickens, stirring continuously. Keep aside to cool. Knead the cottage cheese till it is as smooth as possible, adding a little water if necessary. Blend all the ingredients together in a blender till smooth, adding a little water to obtain the desired spreading or pouring consistency.

■ Meringue Topping

Calories per serving: approx. 20

Take 4 egg whites only, cream of tartar a pinch, salt a pinch, 40 gm icing sugar, 30 gm artificial sweetener or to taste and a few drops vanilla essence.

Beat the egg whites with cream of tartar and salt till fluffy. Fold in the icing sugar and beat again till the mixture is smooth and forms stiff peaks. Add the artificial sweetener and vanilla essence; beat until well mixed. Do not over beat. Use as directed in the recipes.

Note: Refer to tips on beating eggs for maximum volume (see p. 9)

■ Honey Cinnamon Pie Crust

Calories per serving: approx. 76

Take 6 slices of bread, 1½ gm cinnamon (*dalchini*) powder and 30 ml honey or jam of your choice (melted).

Toast the slices of bread and then blend in a blender with cinnamon powder to make breadcrumbs. Spoon out the honey using a spoon dipped in hot water, and add to the breadcrumbs mixing a little at a time. Alternately, melt the jam, cool slightly, and mix it with the breadcrumbs. Press the breadcrumb mixture evenly with the fingertips, moistening the fingers with water if necessary, into the base of a 5″-6″ pie or flan case. Chill a little before adding the filling.

■ Vanilla Ice Cream

Calories per serving: approx. 75

Take 2 eggs, separated, 30 gm cornflour, 600 ml skimmed milk, 50 gm artificial sweetener or to taste, 4-5 drops vanilla essence, 15 gm gelatine, salt and cream of tartar a pinch each.

Beat the egg yolks with cornflour. Stir the skimmed milk into the yolk-cornflour mixture. Cook on a slow fire till it thickens, stirring continuously. Remove from the flame, add the artificial sweetener and vanilla essence. Dissolve the gelatine in a little hot water, and add to the above mixture. Freeze till it sets. Blend once again till fluffy. Beat the egg whites stiffly with salt and cream of tartar. Fold into the ice cream mixture. Freeze till set.

Note: This can also be made in an ice cream maker if you possess one. In which case you do not have to freeze and blend again, instead just fold in the beaten egg whites and pour into the ice cream maker.

Substitutes

The following are a list of ingredients that can be substituted in case of unavailability:

Cream of tartar   This can be substituted with a pinch of salt.

Cornflour   Substitute with twice the amount of refined flour or the same amount of custard powder, though the mixture will be less translucent.

Fresh fruits   Instead of fresh fruits you can use canned fruits dipped in syrup, but drain the syrup and wash the fruits thoroughly in water before use.

Gelatine   This can be substituted with China grass. Take approximately twice the quantity of the required gelatine. (Refer to the instructions on the package.)

Artificial sweetener   Instead of artificial sweetener you can use the tablet variety which dissolves in water.

Blancmange (chocolate milk jelly)

Preparation time: 20 min.
Cooking time: 5 min.
Serves: 2-4
Calories per serving: approx. 60

Ingredients:

Cocoa powder	1 tbsp / 15 gm
Gelatine	3 tsp / 15 gm
Skimmed milk, refrigerated, chilled	1 cup / 200 ml
Vanilla essence	a few drops
Artificial sweetener to taste or	4 tsp / 20 gm
Chocolate, grated for garnishing	1 bar / 40 gm

Method:

1. Grease a mould lightly. Keep aside.
2. Dissolve the gelatine in a little hot water. Add the cocoa powder and mix well. Keep aside to cool.
3. Fold the cocoa mixture into the skimmed milk. Add the vanilla essence and artificial sweetener.
4. Pour the mixture into the prepared mould and refrigerate till set.
5. To serve, dip the mould in hot water for just a few seconds to loosen the sides, then invert on a platter and garnish with chocolate flakes.

Cinnamon Créme with Chocolate Flakes

Preparation time: 20 min.
Cooking time: 35 min.
Serves: 2-4
Calories per serving: approx. 85

Ingredients:

Semolina (*suji*)	1 tbsp / 15 gm
Skimmed milk	1 cup / 200 ml
Coffee powder	2 tsp / 10 gm
Cinnamon (*dalchini*) powder	1 tsp / 5 gm
Artificial sweetener to taste or	8 tsp / 40 gm
Vanilla essence	2-3 drops
Egg, whites only	2
Cream of tartar	a pinch
Salt	a pinch
Plain chocolate, grated for garnishing	1 bar / 40 gm

Method:

1. Powder the semolina in a blender if not already fine; roast slightly till the raw smell disappears.
2. Bring the skimmed milk to a boil; add the semolina and coffee powder, stirring continuously. Cook till the mixture is thickened.
3. Remove from the flame; add cinnamon powder, artificial sweetener and vanilla essence. Keep in the refrigerator to chill.
4. Beat the egg whites with cream of tartar and salt till stiff.
5. Remove the semolina mixture from the refrigerator and gently fold in the egg whites. Serve chilled, garnished with chocolate flakes.

Rich Chocolate Meringue Gateau

Preparation time: 20 min.
Cooking time: 20 min.
Serves: 6-8
Calories per serving: approx. 120

Ingredients:

Chocolate sponge cake (see p. 12)	½
For the filling:	
Cocoa powder	4 tsp / 20 gm
Coffee powder	1 tsp / 5 gm
Water, hot	2 tbsp / 30 ml
Whipped cream (see p. 12)	
Artificial sweetener	to taste
For the topping:	
Meringue topping (see p. 13)	

Method:

1. Scoop out half the cake from the centre of the chocolate sponge leaving a hollow in the centre.
2. For the filling, dissolve the cocoa and coffee powders in hot water; stir into the whipped cream. Add the artificial sweetener. Chill well.
3. Fill the cake hollow with this cocoa-cream mixture.
4. Top with the meringue mixture covering the cocoa cream completely. Place in a preheated oven (225°C) and grill till the meringue is lightly coloured and crisp on top (approximately 4-5 minutes).
5. Serve warm.

Chocolate Lovers' Special

Brownie Cup Cakes

Preparation time: 20 min.
Cooking time: 35 min.
Serves: 8-10
Calories per serving: approx. 97

Ingredients:

Refined flour (*maida*)	1 cup / 100 gm
Cocoa powder	4 tsp / 20 gm
Baking powder	1 tsp / 5 gm
Soda bicarbonate	¼ tsp / 1½ gm
Eggs	2
Sugar	⅓ cup / 50 gm
Ash gourd (*petha*), grated	1 cup / 150 gm
Vanilla essence	a few drops
Coffee powder, dissolved in 3 tbsp of hot water	3 tsp / 15 gm
Vinegar (*sirka*)	2 tbsp / 30 ml

Method:

1. Grease a muffin tray or individual paper cups and dust lightly with flour.
2. Sift the refined flour, cocoa powder, baking powder and soda bicarbonate together.
3. Beat the eggs with sugar till creamy. Add to the flour mixture a little at a time, adding a few spoons of water to obtain a dropping consistency.
4. Squeeze the water out of the ash gourd and add to the above mixture.
5. Add the vanilla essence and the dissolved coffee.
6. Stir in the vinegar just before spooning the mixture into the tray. Bake at 180°C till the cake is done.

Black Forest Trifle

Preparation time: 20 min.
Cooking time: 35 min.
Serves: 2-3
Calories per serving: approx. 169

Ingredients:

Cherries (*gilas*), fresh, stoned	1½ cups / 150 gm
Rum	2 tbsp / 30 ml
White bread, slices	1½
Cinnamon (*dalchini*) powder	a pinch
Whipped cream (see p. 12)	
Chocolate, grated for garnishing	1 bar / 40 gm

Method:

1. Soak the cherries in rum for at least overnight, if not for 2-3 days.
2. Toast the slices of bread slightly; crush them in a blender to form breadcrumbs. Add the cinnamon powder and mix well. Sprinkle this mixture on the bottom of a serving dish.
3. Mix the cherry-rum mixture (reserving a few for garnishing) with the whipped cream. Spoon this mixture over the breadcrumb layer.
4. Garnish with chocolate and cherries.
5. Freeze and serve.

(See photograph on page 4)

Vanilla Ice Cream with Chocolate Fudge Sauce

Preparation time: 20 min.
Cooking time: 35 min.
Serves: 6-8
Calories per serving: approx. 115 (without nuts), 145 (with nuts)

Ingredients:

Vanilla ice cream (see p. 14)

For the chocolate fudge sauce:

Skimmed milk	1 cup / 200 ml
Cocoa powder	1 tbsp / 15 gm
Coffee powder	2 tsp / 10 gm
Vanilla essence	a few drops
Artificial sweetener	to taste

Cashew nuts (*kaju*), finely chopped for garnishing (optional) 2 tsp / 10 gm

Method:

1. Let the vanilla ice cream remain in the freezer until ready to use.
2. For the chocolate fudge sauce, heat the skimmed milk, cocoa powder, coffee powder and vanilla essence in a pan. Stir continuously to avoid the formation of lumps.
3. Cook over a low flame till the sauce becomes thick and creamy. Add the artificial sweetener to taste and remove from the flame.
4. Serve the hot chocolate fudge sauce over a scoop of vanilla ice cream. Garnish with cashew nuts if desired.

Devil's Food Cake

Preparation time: 20 min.
Cooking time: 30 min.
Serves: 6-8
Calories per serving: approx. 177

Ingredients:

Refined flour (*maida*)	1 cup / 100 gm
Baking powder	¾ tsp
Cocoa powder	1 tbsp / 15 gm
Eggs, large	4
Sugar	⅓ cup / 50 gm
Coffee powder	3 tsp / 15 gm
Vinegar (*sirka*)	2 tbsp / 30 ml
Water, boiling hot	¼ cup / 50 ml
Soda bicarbonate	¼ tsp / 1½ gm
For the topping:	
Vanilla essence	¼ tsp / 1½ ml
Whipped cream (see p. 12)	
Chocolate, grated for garnishing (optional)	1 bar / 40 gm

Method:

1. Grease a baking tin and dust lightly with flour.
2. Sift the refined flour, baking powder and cocoa powder together and keep aside.
3. Beat the eggs with sugar till creamy. Add to the flour mixture a few tbsp at a time.
4. Mix the coffee powder, vinegar and soda bicarbonate in boiling water and fold in the above mixture. Transfer the mixture to the prepared tin.
5. Bake in a preheated oven at 180°C for 35 minutes.
6. For the topping, add vanilla essence to the whipped cream, mix well and keep aside. When the cake is done, cool and top with vanilla cream.
7. Garnish with chocolate if desired.

Peach Cups

Preparation time: 10 min.
Cooking time: 3-4 min.
Serves: 2-4
Calories per serving: approx. 116

I n g r e d i e n t s :

Peaches (*arhoo*), large, halved	4
Orange (*santra*) or strawberry (*istabari*) custard powder	2 tsp / 10 gm
Skimmed milk	1 cup / 200 ml
Artificial sweetener	4 tsp / 20 gm
Chocolate, melted	1 bar / 40 gm

M e t h o d :

1. Scoop out the pulp from the peach cups leaving the shells behind. Slice off a small piece at the bottom so that the cups sit firmly on a plate.
2. Shred the peach pulp and set aside.
3. Dissolve the orange or strawberry custard powder in the skimmed milk; cook till it thickens. Cool, stir in the peach pulp and artificial sweetener.
4. Set the shells in goblets. Pour the custard into the shells leaving the top a little empty.
5. Spoon 1 tbsp of the melted chocolate on the top of each peach cup or make chocolate leaves and garnish with the leaves. Chill and serve.

Note: To make chocolate leaves, melt the chocolate in a double boiler at a low temperature. Brush this thickly on the top of fresh lemon leaves. Chill on a sheet of waxed paper till set, then peel off the lemon leaves from the back of the set chocolate. Keep the chocolate leaves frozen in an airtight container. Garnish just before serving.

Chocolate Cream Pie

Preparation time: 20 min.
Cooking time: 3-4 min.
Serves: 4-6
Calories per serving: approx. 146

Ingredients:

Honey cinnamon pie crust (see p. 13)	1
For the filling:	
Cornflour	4 tsp / 20 gm
Skimmed milk	2 cups / 400 ml
Coffee powder	2 tsp / 10 gm
Gelatine	6 tsp / 30 gm
Cocoa powder	4 tsp / 20 gm
Artificial sweetener	to taste
Vanilla essence	2-3 drops
Chocolate essence	2-3 drops
Dates (*khajoor*), shredded for garnishing	¼ cup / 50 gm

Method:

1. Dissolve the cornflour in skimmed milk. Add the coffee powder and cook on a slow flame, stirring continuously, till the mixture thickens. Remove from the flame.
2. Dissolve the gelatine and cocoa powder in a little hot water and add to the coffee mixture.
3. Add the artificial sweetener, vanilla essence and chocolate essence. Mix well. Keep aside to cool.
4. When cool, pour the mixture over the honey cinnamon pie crust.
5. Chill until the mixture sets. Serve garnished with dates.

Chocoberry Dessert

Preparation time: 20 min.
Cooking time: 35 min.
Serves: 4-6
Calories per serving: approx. 60

Ingredients:

Cottage cheese (*paneer*),	1 cup / 100 gm
Strawberries (*istabari*)	1 cup / 150 gm
Water	½ cup / 100 ml
Artificial sweetener	to taste
Strawberry (*istabari*) essence	a few drops
Red food colour (*optional*)	a few drops
Gelatine	2 tsp / 10 gm
Cocoa powder	1 tbsp / 15 gm
Coffee powder	1 tsp / 5 gm
Cornflour	2 tsp / 10 gm
Skimmed milk	1 cup / 200 ml
Vanilla essence	a few drops
Sugar	2 tbsp / 30 gm

Method:

1. Blend the cottage cheese, strawberries and water in a blender till smooth. Add the artificial sweetener, strawberry essence and red food colour. Pour this mixture in a greased mould and freeze.
2. Dissolve the gelatine, cocoa powder and coffee powder in a little hot water. Keep aside.
3. Dissolve the cornflour in skimmed milk and cook till the milk thickens, stirring continuously.
4. Remove from the flame; stir in the gelatine mixture and vanilla essence. Add the sugar, mix well and keep aside. When cool, pour this over the strawberry mixture. Freeze again to set well.
5. Dip the mould in hot water for just a second and invert on a serving platter prior to serving.

Pineapple Cream Cake

Preparation time: 30 min.
Cooking time: 35 min.
Serves: 6-8
Calories per serving: approx. 165

Classic Cakes

Ingredients:

Sponge cake (see p. 11)	1
For the syrup:	
Coffee powder	2 tsp / 10 gm
Water, hot	½ cup / 100 ml
Artificial sweetener	2 tsp / 10 gm
Vanilla essence	2-3 drops
For the pineapple cream filling and topping:	
Whipped cream (see p. 12)	
Pineapple (*ananas*) essence	2-3 drops
Artificial sweetener (optional)	to taste
Pineapple (*ananas*), shredded	1 cup / 150 gm
Grapes (*angoor*), halved	a few
Pineapple (*ananas*), sliced	a few
Raspberries (*rushbary*), halved	a few

Method:

1. Cut the cake horizontally into two halves. Keep both aside.
2. Mix together the syrup ingredients and pour it evenly over the lower half of the sponge cake.
3. For the filling and topping, mix all the ingredients (except the pineapple); spread half of the cream mixture over the lower half of the cake and top with pineapple.
4. Place the second half of the sponge cake over the filling. Spread the remaining cream mixture over it and along the sides.
5. Garnish with grapes, pineapple and raspberries.

Apple Cake

Preparation time: 20 min.
Cooking time: 35 min.
Serves: 8-10
Calories per serving: approx. 132

Ingredients:

Apples (*seb*), diced	2 cups / 300 gm
Refined flour (*maida*)	1 cup / 100 gm
Salt	a pinch
Baking powder	¼ tsp / 1½ gm
Soda bicarbonate	1½ tsp / 8 gm
Cinnamon (*dalchini*) powder	½ tsp / 3 gm
Nutmeg (*jaiphal*) powder	½ tsp / 3 gm
Clove (*laung*) powder	¼ tsp / 1½ gm
Eggs	2
Honey	½ cup / 100 ml
Vanilla essence	¼ tsp / 1½ ml
Vinegar (*sirka*)	1 tbsp / 15 ml

Method:

1. Grease a 9" ring mould and dust with flour.
2. Sift the refined flour, salt, baking powder and soda bicarbonate. Mix in the spices.
3. Beat the eggs till creamy; add the honey and mix well.
4. Fold in the flour mixture, a little at a time. Add 1-3 tbsp of water, if necessary, to obtain a dropping consistency. Add the apples, vanilla essence and vinegar. Mix well. Transfer the cake mixture to the prepared ring mould.
5. Bake at 180°C for around 35 minutes or until the cake is done.

Strawberry Cream Cake

Preparation time: 30 min.
Cooking time: 35 min.
Serves: 6-8
Calories per serving: approx. 164

Ingredients:

Sponge cake (see p. 11)	1

For the strawberry cream:

Strawberries (istabari), washed	1 cup / 150 gm
Whipped cream (see p. 12)	
Strawberry (istabari) essence	a few drops
Red food colouring or beetroot juice (optional)	a few drops
Artificial sweetener, if required	to taste
Strawberries (istabari), sliced for garnishing	a few

Method:

1. Blend the strawberries in a blender till smooth and creamy.
2. Fold in the whipped cream, strawberry essence, red food colouring or beetroot juice and artificial sweetener. Mix well.
3. Spread the strawberry cream over the sponge cake and along the sides. Garnish with strawberries.
4. Serve chilled.

Fruit Cake

Preparation time: 20 min.
Cooking time: 35 min.
Serves: 6-8
Calories per serving: approx. 132.

Ingredients:

Refined flour (*maida*)	1 cup / 100 gm
Baking powder	1¼ tsp / 6⅔ gm
Salt	a pinch
Soda bicarbonate	¼ tsp / 1⅓ gm
Eggs	2
Sugar, powdered	⅓ cup / 50 gm
Medium-calorie fruits, mixed (see p. 10)	1 cup / 150 gm
Carrots (*gajar*), grated	½ cup / 75 gm
Cinnamon (*dalchini*) powder	1 tsp / 5 gm
Orange (*santra*) essence	2-3 drops
Strawberry (*istabari*) essence	2-3 drops
Vinegar (*sirka*)	1 tbsp / 15 ml

Method:

1. Grease a 7"- 8" baking tin; dust lightly with refined flour.
2. Sift the refined flour, baking powder, salt and soda bicarbonate together. Keep aside.
3. Beat the eggs with sugar till creamy.
4. Fold in the flour mixture, a little at a time, adding 1-3 tbsp water, if necessary, to obtain a dropping consistency. Stir in the mixed fruits, carrots, cinnamon powder, orange essence and strawberry essence.
5. Add the vinegar just before transferring the mixture to the prepared tin.
6. Bake at 200°C for about 35 minutes or until the cake is done.

Apricot Cake

Preparation time: 30 min.
Cooking time: 35 min.
Serves: 6-8
Calories per serving: approx. 180

Ingredients :

Sponge cake (see p. 11)	1

For the topping:

Apricots (khumani), dried,	
soaked in hot water	¼ cup / 50 gm
Skimmed milk powder	1 tbsp / 15 gm
Artificial sweetener	to taste

For the filling:

Apricots (khumani), fresh, cut into slices	2-3
Lemon rind (nimbu ka chilka),	
grated	¼ tsp / 3 gm
Artificial sweetener	1 tsp / 5 gm

Method :

1. Cut the cake horizontally into two halves. Keep aside.
2. For the topping, drain the dried apricots and blend in a blender with skimmed milk powder and a little water till the mixture is smooth and creamy.
3. Sweeten with a little artificial sweetener, if required, and keep aside.
4. For the filling, mix the fresh apricots with the lemon rind and artificial sweetener.
5. Layer the lower half of the cake with fresh apricot mixture.
6. Place the other half of the cake on top. Smooth the apricot cream on top and along the sides of the cake and serve.

Orange-Lemon Cake

Preparation time: 30 min.
Cooking time: 35 min.
Serves: 6-8
Calories per serving: approx. 158

Ingredients:

Sponge or orange cake
(see p. 11 or 12)   1

For the topping:

Orange (santra) marmalade   3 tbsp / 45 gm
Orange pulp, shredded   1 cup / 150 gm
Orange and lemon (nimbu)
rind, mixed   2 tsp / 10 gm
Artificial sweetener (optional)   to taste
Orange and lemon, thin slices   a few

Method:

1. Dissolve the orange marmalade in a little hot water.
2. Stir in the orange pulp, mixed orange and lemon rinds and artificial sweetener if required.
3. Spread this mixture on top of the sponge or orange cake.
4. Serve, garnished with orange and lemon slices.

Pumpkin Spice Cake

Preparation time: 20 min.
Cooking time: 35 min.
Serves: 6-8
Calories per serving: approx. 100

Ingredients:

Sponge cake (see p. 11)	½
Pumpkin (*kaddu*), grated	2 cups / 300 gm
Nutmeg (*jaiphal*) powder	¼ tsp / 1½ gm
Cinnamon (*dalchini*) powder	¼ tsp / 1½ gm
Clove (*laung*) powder	¼ tsp / 1½ gm
Refined flour (*maida*)	4 tsp / 20 gm
Vanilla essence	¼ tsp / 1½ ml
Juice of lemon (*nimbu*)	1
Lemon rind (*nimbu ka chilka*)	2 tsp / 10 gm

Method:

1. Scoop out the centre of the sponge cake carefully leaving a hollow shell.
2. Cook the pumpkin with a little water till soft. Keep aside to cool.
3. Purée the pumpkin in a blender.
4. Heat the puréed pumpkin in a pan; add the spices and refined flour dissolved in a little water and cook till the mixture thickens.
5. Cool, and add the lemon juice and rind.
6. Fill the cake shell with this pumpkin mixture, and smoothen the top. Refrigerate until set.
7. Serve chilled.

Mango Mousse Cake

Preparation time: 40 min.
Cooking time: 35 min.
Serves: 6-8
Calories per serving: approx. 95

Ingredients:

Sponge cake (see p. 11)   ½
For the mango mousse topping:
Papaya (*papita*), puréed   ½ cup / 75 ml
Ice cubes   8-10
Skimmed milk powder   1 tbsp / 15 gm
Gelatine, dissolved in hot
   water   6 tsp / 30 gm
Lemon (*nimbu*) juice   2 tbsp / 30 ml
Mango (*aam*) essence   a few drops
Artificial sweetener   to taste
Orange or yellow food colour (optional)

Method:

1. For the topping, freeze the papaya purée in ice-cube trays. When frozen, crush these cubes and the plain ice cubes in a blender for a few minutes.
2. Dissolve the skimmed milk powder in a little water and add to the above mixture. Blend for a minute. Add gelatine, lemon juice, mango essence, artificial sweetener and orange or yellow colour. Blend till thick and creamy. Freeze till ready to use.
3. Fold a sheet of greased-butter paper into a long strip, and arrange it like a collar around the cake, adding more height. Secure it with a pin. Fill the collar with the mixture. Chill until firm. Remove the collar and serve frozen, if desired.

Lemon Snow Cake

Preparation time: 35 min.
Cooking time: 35 min.
Serves: 6-8
Calories per serving: approx. 98

Ingredients:

Sponge cake (see p. 11)	½
For the lemon snow topping:	
Skimmed milk	2 cups / 400 ml
Refined flour (*maida*)	4 tsp / 20 gm
Gelatine, mixed in hot water	6 tsp / 30 gm
Juice of lemons (*nimbu*)	2
Lemon rind (*nimbu ka chilka*), grated	1 tsp / 5 gm
Lemon (*nimbu*) essence (optional)	2-3 drops
Artificial sweetener	to taste
Egg, whites only	4
Salt	a pinch
Cream of tartar	a pinch

Method:

1. Add the refined flour to the skimmed milk. Bring it to a boil, and simmer till thick. Remove from the flame. Add the gelatine, stir till it dissolves.
2. When the milk mixture cools a little, add the lemon juice, rind, essence and artificial sweetener.
3. Put the lemon mixture in the freezer; when it is almost set remove and whip till it is smooth.
4. Whip the egg whites with salt and cream of tartar. Fold into the lemon mixture carefully and chill again till it is nearly firm.
5. Top the sponge cake with this lemon mixture and serve. Keep refrigerated.

Note: Refer tip on beating egg whites (see p. 9).

Marble Cake

Preparation time: 25 min.
Cooking time: 45 min.
Serves: 14-16
Calories per serving: approx. 120

Ingredients:

Refined flour (*maida*)	2 cups / 200 gm
Baking powder	1½ tsp / 8 gm
Baking soda	¼ tsp / 1½ gm
Cocoa powder	2 tbsp / 30 gm
Eggs	6
Sugar	2/3 cup / 100 gm
Strawberry (*istabari*) or	
orange (*santra*) essence	¼ tsp / 1½ ml
Vanilla essence	¼ tsp / 1½ ml
Red or orange food	
colour (optional)	a few drops
Vinegar (*sirka*)	1 tbsp / 15 ml

Method:

1. Grease a 12"-14" baking tin and dust lightly with flour. Keep aside.
2. Sift the refined flour with baking powder and baking soda together. Divide this mixture into 2 halves.
3. Add the cocoa powder to one-half of the flour mixture and sift this mixture again.
4. Beat the eggs with sugar, over a pan of hot water, till thick and creamy. Divide the egg mixture into 2 halves.
5. Fold in the cocoa mixture into one-half of the egg mixture, a few tbsp at a time. Add 2 tbsp of water, if necessary, to obtain a dropping consistency.

6. Stir in the vanilla essence and vinegar.
7. Fold in the plain flour mixture into the other half of the egg mixture, a few tbsp at a time. Add water, if necessary, to obtain a dropping consistency. Stir in the strawberry or orange essence and red or orange food colour.

8. Drop alternate spoonfuls of the cocoa and the plain flour mixture into the greased tin. Run a knife back and forth through the mixture to give a marbled effect.
9. Bake at 180°C for about 45 minutes, or till the cake is well risen.
10. Cut into slices and serve.

Beat it Right
If you beat the egg in a wet bowl,
the yolk will not stick to the sides and
you will avoid wastage.

Lemon Vanilla Parfait

Preparation time: 25 min.
Cooking time: 15 min.
Serves: 6-8
Calories per serving: approx. 41

Ingredients:

Vanilla custard powder	4 tsp / 20 gm
Gelatin, dissolved in 3 tbsp water	6 tsp / 30 gm
Water	2 cups / 400 ml
Juice of lemons (*nimbu*)	2
Artificial sweetener	5½ tbsp / 80 gm
Skimmed milk	2 cups / 400 ml
Lemon rind (*nimbu ka chilka*), grated	2 tsp / 10 gm
Lemon essence (optional)	a few drops
Vanilla essence	a few drops
Skimmed milk powder	3 tbsp / 45 gm
Egg, whites only	4
Salt	a pinch
Cream of tartar	a pinch

Method:

1. Dissolve the vanilla custard powder in water, and cook till thick, stirring continuously.
2. Remove this from the fire and stir in the gelatine. Cool slightly, add all the ingredients till vanilla essence. Mix well. The mixture should taste lemony so add extra lemon juice or lemon essence if needed.
3. Freeze the mixture in ice-cube trays till set. Blend the frozen cubes in a blender with skimmed milk powder till soft and fluffy.
4. Beat the egg whites with cream of tartar and salt till stiff. Fold the lemon mixture into the egg whites.
5. Freeze till set and serve in goblets or parfait glasses.

Thandai
Frozen flavoured milk

Preparation time: 10 min.
Cooking time: 35 min.
Serves: 2-4
Calories per serving: approx. 70

Ingredients:

Skimmed milk	1 cup / 200 ml
Cornflour	1 tsp / 5 gm
Black pepper (*kali mirch*) powder	¼ tsp / 1½ gm
Poppy seeds (*khuskhus*), roasted, powdered	1 tsp / 5 gm
Aniseed (*saunf*), roasted, powdered	1 tsp / 5 gm
Rum	1 tbsp / 15 ml
Gelatine, dissolved in a little hot water	3 tsp / 15 gm
Artificial sweetener to taste or	4 tsp / 20 gm
Rose water (*gulab jal*)	¼ tsp / 1½ ml
Vetiver (*kewda*) essence	¼ tsp / 1½ ml
Almond (*badam*) essence	a few drops

Method:

1. Dissolve the cornflour in skimmed milk; add the black pepper, poppy seed and aniseed powders. Cook for 2-3 minutes till the milk thickens a little.
2. Remove from the flame, stir in the rum, gelatine dissolved in hot water, artificial sweetener, rose water, vetiver and almond essences till well mixed.
3. Chill in a dish till set and serve.

Mango Kulfi

Mango ice cream

Preparation time: 15 min.
Cooking time: 10 min.
Serves: 4-6
Calories per serving: approx. 55

Ingredients:

Water, hot	1 cup / 200 ml
Gelatine, dissolved in 2 tbsp hot water	2 tsp / 10 gm
Cornflour	2 tsp / 10 gm
Skimmed milk	1 cup / 200 ml
Papaya (*papita*), puréed	1 cup / 150 gm
Pistachios (*pista*), chopped	2 tbsp / 20 gm
Mango (*aam*) essence	¼ tsp / 1½ ml
Lemon (*nimbu*) juice	1 tbsp / 15 ml
Almond (*badam*) essence	a few drops
Vetiver (*kewda*) essence	a few drops
Saffron (*kesar*), soaked in 2 tbsp milk	a few strands
Orange food colour (optional)	a few drops
Artificial sweetener to taste or	8 tsp / 40 gm
Ice cubes	8-10

Method:

1. Heat the water in a pan; add the gelatine mixture. Stir till the gelatine is completely dissolved. Keep aside.
2. Dissolve the cornflour in skimmed milk, bring to a boil. Stir till the milk thickens slightly. Mix in the gelatine mixture; remove from the flame. Cool.
3. Add the remaining ingredients to it and blend till thick and creamy.
4. Freeze till the mixture sets. Blend once again and refreeze in *kulfi* moulds.
5. To serve, invert the moulds on to individual bowls.

Chenna Payas
Cottage cheese dumplings in flavoured milk

Preparation time: 30 min.
Cooking time: 20 min.
Serves: 1-2
Calories per serving: approx. 115

Ingredients:

Soft cottage cheese (*chenna*), made
   from skimmed milk   1 cup / 100 gm
Skimmed milk   1 cup / 200 ml
Cornflour   1 tsp / 5 gm
Green cardamom
   (*choti elaichi*) powder   ¼ tsp / 1½ gm
Artificial sweetener   4 tsp / 20 gm
Saffron (*kesar*), dissolved in
   warm milk   a few strands

Method:

1. Knead the cottage cheese well to make a smooth dough. Divide the dough into small balls. Keep aside.
2. Dissolve the cornflour in the skimmed milk, and bring to a boil.
3. Slide the cottage cheese balls in the milk and cook for a minute or two.
4. Stir in the green cardamom powder, artificial sweetener and saffron.
5. Serve chilled.

Sheera
Wholewheat porridge

Preparation time: 5 min.
Cooking time: 15 min.
Serves: 4-6
Calories per serving: approx. 63

Ingredients:

Wholewheat flour (*atta*)	3 tsp / 15 gm
Clarified butter (*ghee*)	1 tsp / 5 gm
Skimmed milk	3 cups / 600 ml
Green cardamom	
(*choti elaichi*) powder	¼ tsp / 1½ gm
Artificial sweetener to taste or	4 tsp / 20 gm

Method:

1. Roast the wholewheat flour with clarified butter till it is golden brown and the raw smell disappears.
2. Add the skimmed milk, stirring continuously to avoid the formation of lumps. Cook for a few minutes.
3. Stir in the green cardamom powder and add artificial sweetener to taste.
4. Serve hot or cold in silver or clay bowls.

Gajar Ka Halwa
Carrot delight

Preparation time: 20 min.
Cooking time: 35 min.
Serves: 2-4
Calories per serving: approx.112

Ingredients:

Carrots (*gajar*), grated	500 gm
Skimmed milk	3 cups / 600 ml
Raisins (*kishmish*), chopped	2 tsp / 10 gm
Artificial sweetener	8 tsp / 40 gm
Green cardamom	
(*choti elaichi*) powder	¼ tsp / 1½ gm
Clarified butter (*ghee*), melted	2 tsp / 10 gm

Method:

1. Cook the carrots with skimmed milk in a large heavy-bottomed pan till the milk evaporates.
2. Remove from the flame; add the raisins, artificial sweetener and green cardamom powder. Mix well.
3. Serve warm or chilled, topped with ½ tsp clarified butter per serving.

Selecting Carrots
The deeper the colour of the carrot,
the better the source of vitamin A.

Fruit Cup with Almond Cream

Preparation time: 20 min.
Serves: 4-6
Calories per serving: approx. 87 (with cream)
53 calories (without cream)

Ingredients:

Papaya (*papita*), chopped	2 cups / 300 gm
Medium-calorie fruits (see p. 10), mixed, chopped	2 cups / 300 gm
Juice of lemon (*nimbu*)	1
Rum	2 tbsp / 30 ml
Almond (*badam*) essence	2-3 drops
Whipped cream (see p. 12)	
Artificial sweetener, if required,	to taste

Method:

1. Mix together the fruits, lemon juice and rum. Refrigerate for at least 3 days to develop the flavour.
2. Stir in the almond essence into the whipped cream. Keep aside.
3. Serve the almond cream topped with fruits (add artificial sweetener if required).

Tutti-frutti

Fresh Fruit Meringue

Preparation time: 45 min.
Cooking time: 5 min.
Serves: 6-8
Calories per serving: approx. 70

Tutti-frutti

Ingredients:

Meringue topping (see p. 13)
For the fresh fruits:

Papaya (*papita*), chopped	1 cup / 150 gm
Pineapple (*ananas*), shredded	1 cup / 150 gm
Apple (*seb*), finely chopped	1 cup / 150 gm
Mixed fruits (see p. 10), chopped	1 cup / 150 gm
Lemon (*nimbu*) juice	2 tbsp / 30 ml
Artificial sweetener	4 tsp / 20 gm

Method:

1. Mix the fruits with lemon juice and artificial sweetener. Keep aside to chill.
2. Spread half the meringue mixture on a greased rectangular foil sheet, placed on a tray.
3. Add the chilled fruit mixture over half the meringue mixture.
4. Spread the remaining meringue on top, ensuring that the fruits are well covered.
5. Bake on the top shelf of a preheated oven (225°C) for 4-5 minutes, till delicately coloured and crisp on top.
6. Serve immediately while the meringue is warm.

Note: The fruits should be well chilled, and completely covered with the meringue so that they remain cold and uncooked, while the meringue is warm. You can also make individual servings in any shape you desire.

Caramel Brown Bread with Ice Cream

Preparation time: 30 min.
Cooking time: 15 min.
Serves: 4-6
Calories per serving: approx. 135

Ingredients:

Vanilla ice cream (see p. 14)
For the brown bread topping:

Brown bread, slices	3
Sugar	3 tsp / 15 gm
Vanilla essence	a few drops

Method:

1. Toast the slices of bread lightly, and crush in a blender till fine breadcrumbs are obtained.
2. Heat the breadcrumbs with the sugar on a slow fire, stirring till the sugar caramelises and coats the crumbs.
3. Remove from the fire, and stir in the vanilla essence.
4. Serve the vanilla ice cream topped with brown breadcrumb mixture. Alternately, arrange layers of ice cream and bread praline in individual bowls before serving.

Cheesecake

Preparation time: 20 min.
Serves: 4-6
Calories per serving: approx. 110

Ingredients:

Honey cinnamon pie crust (see p. 13)	1
Whipped cream (see p. 12)	
Gelatine, dissolved in a little hot water	5 tsp / 25 gm
Lemon (*nimbu*) juice	1 tbsp / 15 ml
Lemon rind (*nimbu ka chilka*), grated	½ tsp / 3 gm

Method:

1. Stir the dissolved gelatine into the whipped cream until well blended.
2. Add the lemon juice and rind, adding more to taste, if necessary. Chill slightly.
3. Pour the cheesecake mixture into the honey cinnamon pie crust and refrigerate till set.
4. Serve chilled.

Tutti-frutti

Toffee Apple Rings

Preparation time: 15 min.
Cooking time: 15 min.
Serves: 2-4
Calories per serving: approx. 88

Tutti-frutti

Ingredients:

Apple (*seb*), large, cored, cut into rings	1
Juice of lemon (*nimbu*)	1
Sugar	4 tsp / 20 gm
Vanilla essence	2-3 drops
Vanilla custard powder	2 tsp / 10 gm
Skimmed milk	1 cup / 200 ml
Brown food colour (optional)	a few drops
Artificial sweetener to taste or	1 tsp / 5 gm

Method:

1. Rub the apple rings with lemon juice and keep aside in the refrigerator to chill.
2. Heat the sugar with 2 tsp water on a low flame till a toffee or caramel colour is obtained.
3. Add 1-2 tbsp water, stirring continuously. Remove from the heat. Mix in the vanilla essence. Keep aside.
4. Dissolve the vanilla custard powder in the skimmed milk. Cook till thick, adding any leftover apple bits.
5. Stir in the sugar mixture, brown food colour if required and artificial sweetener to taste.
6. Serve the chilled apple rings topped with warm toffee sauce.

Apple Crumble

Preparation time: 10 min.
Cooking time: 15 min.
Serves: 4-5
Calories per serving: approx. 133

Ingredients:

Apples (*seb*), thinly sliced	4
Juice of lemon (*nimbu*)	1
Vanilla essence	¼ tsp / 1½ ml
Jam of your choice	4 tsp / 20 gm
Dry ginger powder (*sonth*)	½ tsp / 3 gm
All spice powder	a pinch
For the crumble mixture:	
Bread, slices	2
Cinnamon (*dalchini*) powder	a pinch
Artificial sweetener	to taste
Butter (*makhan*), melted	2 tsp / 10 ml
Orange (*santra*) or lemon (*nimbu*) juice, fresh (optional)	a few spoons
Cornflakes, slightly crushed	2 tbsp / 30 gm

Method:

1. Add the lemon juice and vanilla essence to the apples. Mix and keep aside.

2. Melt the jam in a pan, adding a little water. Add the spices to the hot jam mixture, warm slightly then remove from the flame. Coat the apples with the jam mixture and arrange on a serving dish.

3. For the crumble mixture, toast the slices of bread till golden. Cool and blend till coarse breadcrumbs are obtained. Stir in the cinnamon powder, artificial sweetener and butter. If you prefer a moist crumble, add a few tsp of orange or lemon juice.

4. Add the cornflakes to the above mixture just before serving. Sprinkle the warm crumble mixture over the apples and serve.

Rum and Raisin Oranges

Preparation time: 20 min.
Serves: 2-4
Calories per serving: approx. 95
130 (with walnuts and cream)

Ingredients:

Oranges (*santra*), large, halved	2
Raisins (*kishmish*)	4 tsp / 20 gm
Rum	2 tbsp / 30 ml
Orange (*santra*) and lemon (*nimbu*) rinds, grated	1 tsp / 5 gm
Artificial sweetener to taste or	4 tsp / 20 gm
Walnuts (*akhrot*), lightly toasted, chopped (optional)	2 tsp / 10 gm
Cream	1½ tsp / 8 ml

Method:

1. Scoop out the pulp from the orange halves and deseed. Retain the orange shells.
2. To the orange pulp stir in the raisins, rum, and orange and lemon rinds.
3. Fill the orange shells with this mixture and chill these cups for at least 12 hours to develop the flavour.
4. Add the artificial sweetener and walnuts or top with cream, if required, just before serving. Serve chilled.

Tutti-frutti

Orange Sorbet

Preparation time: 10 min.
Cooking time: 10 min.
Serves: 2-4
Calories per serving: approx. 4

Tutti-frutti

Ingredients:

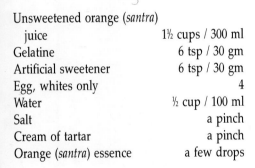

Unsweetened orange (*santra*)
    juice   1½ cups / 300 ml
Gelatine   6 tsp / 30 gm
Artificial sweetener   6 tsp / 30 gm
Egg, whites only   4
Water   ½ cup / 100 ml
Salt   a pinch
Cream of tartar   a pinch
Orange (*santra*) essence   a few drops

Method:

1. Add the gelatine to a few tbsp of water and keep aside for 10 minutes. Heat gently till the gelatine dissolves.
2. Mix the gelatine and artificial sweetener in the unsweetened orange juice. Freeze till half frozen.
3. Beat the half frozen mixture well in a large bowl or blend till creamy.
4. Whip the egg whites with salt, cream of tartar and orange essence till stiff.
5. Fold into the orange juice mixture. Freeze the mixture in a container till it sets. Serve frozen in individual goblets.

Strawberry Sorbet

Preparation time: 10 min.
Cooking time: 2 min.
Serves: 4-6
Calories per serving: approx. 34

Ingredients:

Strawberries (*istabari*),
chopped — 3 cups / 450 gm
Gelatine — 8 tsp / 40 gm
Water — 1 cup / 200 ml
Vanilla essence — a few drops
Artificial sweetener — 6 tsp / 30 gm
Egg, whites only — 4
Cream of tartar — a pinch
Salt — a pinch

Method:

1. Add the gelatine in the water and keep aside for 10 minutes. Heat the mixture gently till it dissolves.
2. Meanwhile, purée the strawberries in a blender till smooth and creamy. Fold the gelatine mixture into the strawberry purée; add the vanilla essence and artificial sweetener.
3. Freeze this mixture in ice-cube trays till it sets.
4. Blend the strawberry cubes in a blender till creamy. Keep aside.
5. Whip the egg whites with cream of tartar and salt till thick and creamy.
6. Fold into the strawberry mixture gently and refreeze in a container till set. Serve frozen in individual goblets.

Tutti-frutti

Cinnamon Fruit Fritters

Preparation time: 10 min.
Cooking time: 15 min.
Serves: 2-4
Calories per serving: approx. 60

Ingredients:

Refined flour (*maida*)	1 cup / 100 gm
Salt	to taste
Baking powder	½ tsp / 3 gm
Apple (*seb*), chopped	1
Medium-calorie fruits, chopped (guavas, pineapple, strawberries)	½ cup / 75 gm
Sugar	3 tsp / 15 gm
Skimmed milk	1 cup / 200 ml
Oil	2 tsp / 10 ml
Artificial sweetener, powdered	2 tsp / 10 gm
Cinnamon (*dalchini*) powder	1 tsp / 5 gm

Method:

1. Sift the refined flour with salt and baking powder.
2. Add the apples, medium-calorie fruits, sugar and skimmed milk. Make a creamy batter.
3. Grease a large non-stick pan; heat and drop spoonfuls of the creamy batter. Fry evenly on both sides till golden brown.
4. Serve the fritters warm, sprinkled with a mixture of artificial sweetener and cinnamon powder.

Tutti-frutti

Apple Kheer
Apple pudding

Preparation time: 10 min.
Cooking time: 30 min.
Serves: 4-6
Calories per serving: approx. 109

Ingredients:

Apples (*seb*), puréed	500 gm
Cornflour	1 tbsp / 15 gm
Skimmed milk	3 cups / 600 ml
Raisins (*kishmish*)	4 tsp / 20 gm
Green cardamom	
(*choti elaichi*) powder	1 tsp / 5 gm
Nutmeg (*jaiphal*) powder	a pinch

Method:

1. Dissolve the cornflour in skimmed milk. Bring to a boil, stirring continuously. Cook for one or two minutes till the milk thickens.
2. Add the apple purée, raisins, green cardamom powder and nutmeg powder. Stir gently for a few minutes till the apple purée is cooked.
3. Serve chilled.

Apples Unpaired
Apples keep longer if they
do not touch one another.

Phirni
Rice pudding

Preparation time: 15 min.
Cooking time: 10 min.
Serves: 2-4
Calories per serving: approx. 80

Ingredients:

Skimmed milk	2 cups / 400 ml
Rice flour	1 tbsp / 15 gm
Almond (*badam*) essence	a few drops
Artificial sweetener	to taste
Green cardamom (*choti elaichi*) powder	½ tsp / 3 gm
Mixed cashew nuts-raisins (*kaju-kishmish*), chopped	2 tbsp / 30 gm

Method:

1. Dissolve the rice flour in the skimmed milk and cook till the milk thickens.
2. Add the almond essence, artificial sweetener and green cardamom powder. Stir till it blends well.
3. Pour this mixture in a serving dish or individual bowls and chill. The *phirni* sets best in clay bowls.
4. Serve, garnished with cashew nuts and raisins.

Stocking Nuts
*Stock nuts that are not salty as these
keep better than the salted ones.*

Sandesh
Soft cottage cheese fudge

Preparation time: 20 min.
Cooking time: 15 min.
Serves: 2-4
Calories per serving: approx. 70

Ingredients:

Soft cottage cheese (*chenna*), from skimmed milk, crumbled	1 cup / 100 gm
Sugar	2 tbsp / 30 gm
Rose water (*gulab jal*)	½ tsp / 3 ml
Artificial sweetener	to taste
Cold water	to knead
Raisins (*kishmish*), for garnishing, optional	a few

Method:

1. Heat the sugar with 1 tbsp water till rich and caramel coloured. Add 1-2 tbsp water and remove from the flame.
2. Blend the caramel and cottage cheese in the blender. Add the rose water and artificial sweetener. Knead the mixture with cold water till the dough is smooth.
3. Roll the dough into small balls and flatten slightly. Place a raisin in the centre of each piece of fudge.
4. Serve at room temperature. When refrigerated, the fudge will stay fresh for 3-4 days.

Gur Dosa
Jaggery pancakes

Preparation time: 10 min.
Cooking time: 20 min.
Serves: 6-8
Calories per serving: approx. 140

Ingredients:

Jaggery (*gur*), grated	1 tbsp / 15 gm
Water	1 cup / 200 ml
Refined flour (*maida*)	¾ cup / 75 gm
Rice flour, finely ground	¼ cup / 25 gm
Lemon (*nimbu*)	½
Oil	4 tsp / 20 ml
Coconut (*nariyal*) powder	4 tsp / 20 gm
Artificial sweetener to taste (optional)	
Green cardamom (*choti elaichi*) powder	½ tsp / 3 gm
Clarified butter (*ghee*) or white butter	4 tsp / 20 gm

Method:

1. Put the jaggery in the water and let it dissolve. Add both the flours, a little at a time, and blend into a smooth batter.
2. Heat a small non-stick pan and rub the surface lightly with half a lemon dipped in very little oil.
3. Pour a ladleful of the batter, tilting the pan to help the mixture spread evenly. Sprinkle some oil and cook on both the sides till golden brown.
4. Mix the coconut powder with artificial sweetener and green cardamom powder. Sprinkle a little of this over the pancakes and roll into cylinders.
5. Brush each roll with ½ tsp melted clarified butter or top with ½ tsp lightly whipped white butter.
6. Serve warm.

Health Punch

Preparation time: 10 min. Serves: 3
Calories per serving: approx. 35

Ingredients:

Cucumber (*khira*) juice	1 cup / 200 ml
Unsweetened orange (*santra*) juice	1 cup / 200 ml
Juice of lemon (*nimbu*)	½
Water	1 cup / 200 ml
Rock salt	a pinch
Mint (*pudina*) leaves, for garnishing	a sprig

Method:

1. Mix all the ingredients together in a jug.
2. Serve chilled in tall glasses, garnished with mint leaves.

Apple-ginger Ale

Preparation time: 5 min. Serves: 1
Calories per serving: approx. 40

Ingredients:

Unsweetened apple (*seb*) juice	½ cup / 100 ml
Ginger (*adrak*) juice, fresh	1 tsp / 5 ml
Lemon (*nimbu*) juice	1 tbsp / 15 ml
Artificial sweetener to taste or	2 tsp / 10 gm
Bottled soda, chilled	½ cup / 100 ml
Salt	a pinch

Method:

1. Mix the unsweetened apple juice, ginger juice, lemon juice and artificial sweetener in a tall glass.
2. Pour the soda on top, and add a dash of salt.
3. Serve chilled.

Strawberry Daiquiri Shake

Preparation time: 7 min. Serves: 2
Calories per serving: approx. 85

Ingredients:

Strawberries (*istabari*), chopped	1 cup / 150 gm
Skimmed milk powder	3 tsp / 15 gm
Rum	2 tbsp / 30 ml
Juice of lemon (*nimbu*)	1
Artificial sweetener	5 tsp / 25 gm
Ice cubes	6-8

Method:

1. Blend all the ingredients in a blender till thick and creamy.
2. Carefully pour the mixture into a salt-rimmed glass without touching the frosted rim.
3. Serve immediately.

Ice Cream Soda

Preparation time: 5 min. Serves: 1
Calories per serving: approx. 38

Ingredients:

Artificial sweetener	2 tsp / 10 gm
Juice of lemon (*nimbu*)	1
Vanilla essence and green colour	a few drops
Bottled soda, chilled	1 cup / 200 ml
Vanilla ice cream (see p. 14)	

Method:

1. Mix the artificial sweetener, lemon juice, vanilla essence and green colour in a glass.
2. Pour the soda, stirring till well mixed.
3. Add the vanilla ice cream and serve immediately.

Spiced Tea Wine

Preparation time: 5 min. Serves: 3
Calories per serving: approx. 27

Ingredients:

Tea leaves	½ tsp / 3 gm
Boiling water	2 cups / 400 ml
Red wine	1 cup / 100 ml
Cinnamon-nutmeg (*dalchini-jaiphal*) powder, mixed	¼ tsp / 1½ gm
Artificial sweetener	3 tsp / 15 gm
Lemon (*nimbu*) juice	3 tbsp / 45 ml

Method:

1. Steep the tea leaves in boiling water for a few minutes. Strain and keep aside.
2. Mix the remaining ingredients in a jug. Add the tea liquor and stir well. Serve chilled.

Café Brulot

Preparation time: 10 min. Cooking time: 5 min. Serves: 1
Calories per serving: approx. 78

Ingredients:

Coffee powder	½ tsp / 3 gm
Artificial sweetener to taste or	2 tsp / 10 gm
Vanilla essence	3-4 drops
Hot water	1 cup / 200 ml
Whipped cream, fresh	1 tsp / 5 gm
Brandy	1 tbsp / 15 ml

Method:

1. Mix the coffee powder, artificial sweetener, vanilla essence in hot water.
2. Float fresh whipped cream on top.
3. Carefully ignite the brandy in a large ladle and pour over the coffee mixture. Serve hot.

Cold Coffee

Preparation time: 5 min. Serves: 1
Calories per serving: approx. 36

Ingredients:

Coffee	1 tbsp / 15 gm
Skimmed milk powder	2 tsp / 10 gm
Artificial sweetener	to taste
Vanilla essence	a few drops
Ice cubes	4-5

Method:

1. Combine all the ingredients together.
2. Blend the mixture in a blender until thick and creamy.
3. Pour into tall glasses and serve immediately.

Strawberry Smoothie

Preparation time: 5 min. Serves: 1
Calories per serving: approx. 35

Ingredients:

Strawberries (*istabari*), chopped, frozen overnight	½ cup / 75 gm
Ice cubes	4-5
Strawberry essence	a few drops
Artificial sweetener	2 tsp / 10 gm

Method:

1. Combine all the ingredients together.
2. Blend the mixture in a blender until thick and smooth. Pour into a tall glass and serve chilled.

Thick Mixed Fruit Shake

Preparation time: 5 min. Serves: 2
Calories per serving: approx. 70

Ingredients:

Mixed fruit, chopped (see p. 10)	1 cup / 150 gm
Skimmed milk powder	2 tsp / 10 gm
Fruit essence of your choice	a few drops
Artificial sweetener to taste or	4 tsp / 20 gm
Ice cubes	6-8

Method:

1. Combine all the ingredients together.
2. Blend the mixture in a blender until thick and creamy.
3. Pour into tall glasses and serve immediately.

Chocolate Milk Shake

Preparation time: 5 min. Serves: 2
Calories per serving: approx. 45

Ingredients:

Skimmed milk powder	3 tsp / 15 gm
Cocoa powder	2 tsp / 10 gm
Coffee powder	1 tsp / 5 gm
Vanilla essence	2-3 drops
Artificial sweetener to taste	4 tsp / 20 gm
Ice cubes	6-8

Method:

1. Combine all the ingredients together.
2. Blend the mixture in a blender till thick and creamy, adding a little additional water if required.
3. Pour into tall glasses and serve immediately.

Glossary of Cooking Terms

Batter — A mixture of flour, liquid and sometimes other ingredients, of a thin, creamy consistency.

Blend — To mix together thoroughly two or more ingredients.

Caramel — Sugar heated to a rich brown sugar syrup.

Coat — To cover food that is to be fried with flour, egg and breadcrumbs or batter.

Curdle — To separate milk or sauce into curds and whey by acid or excessive heat.

Dot — To scatter bits, as of butter or margarine, over the surface of food.

Dough — A thick mixture of uncooked flour and liquid, often combined with other ingredients: the mixture can be handled as a solid mass.

Dust — To sprinkle lightly with flour, sugar, spices or seasonings.

Fold in — To combine a light, whisked or creamed mixture with other ingredients so that it retains its lightness. Usually done with a metal spoon or a rubber spatula.

Fritter — A portion of batter-coated food, deep-fried until crisp.

Fry — To cook in hot fat or oil. In the case of shallow frying only a small quantity of fat is used, in a shallow pan. The food must be turned halfway through to cook both sides. In the case of deep frying, sufficient fat is used to cover the food completely.

Knead	—	To work a dough by hand or machine until smooth.
Meringue	—	Egg white whisked until stiff, mixed with sugar and baked until crisp.
Parfait	—	A light, cream-enriched, iced dessert often made with a fruit purée.
Purée	—	To press food through a fine sieve or blend in a blender or food processor, to a smooth, thick mixture.
Rub in	—	To incorporate the fat into flour using the fingertips; used mainly for shortcrust pastry and plain cakes.
Sift	—	To shake a dry ingredient through a sieve or flour sifter, to remove lumps.
Steam	—	To cook food in steam. Generally food to be steamed is put in a perforated container which is placed above a pan of boiling water.
Syrup	—	A concentrated solution of sugar in water.
Whip	—	To beat rapidly, to introduce air into a mixture; usually of cream.
Whisk	—	To beat rapidly to introduce air into a light mixture; usually of egg.

Index

ISBN: 978-81-7436-155-4

© **This edition Roli & Janssen BV 2008**

Sixth impression
Published in India by Roli Books in
arrangement with Roli & Janssen BV, The Netherlands
M-75 Greater Kailash II (Market) New Delhi 110 048, India
Ph: ++91-11-29212271, 29212782, Fax: ++91-11-29217185
E-mail: roli@vsnl.com, Website: rolibooks.com

Photographs: Dheeraj Paul

Printed and bound in India